Let's Celebrate Series

Fireworks and Freedom

A Fourth of July Story and Activity Book

Story by Carol Amato
Activities by Ann D. Koffsky
Illustrated by Nancy Lane

D1377919

BARRON'S

All inquiries should be addressed to:
Barron's Educational Series, Inc.
250 Wireless Boulevard
Hauppauge, New York 11788
http: //www.barronseduc.com

ISBN-13: 978-0-7641-3567-5
ISBN-10: 0-7641-3567-8

Library of Congress Catalog Card No. 2006042848

Library of Congress Cataloging-in-Publication Data

Amato, Carol A.
    Fireworks and Freedom: A Fourth of July Story and Activity Book / story
by Carol Amato; activities by Ann D. Koffsky; illustrated by Nancy Lane.
        p.   cm. —(Let's celebrate series)
    ISBN-13: 978-0-7641-3567-5
    ISBN-10: 0-7641-3567-8
    1. Fourth of July—Juvenile literature.   2. Fourth of July celebrations—
Juvenile literature.   I. Koffsky, Ann D.   II. Lane, Nancy, 1960–ill.   III. Title.
IV. Series.

E286.A115   2007
394.2634—dc22   2006042848

Printed in China
9 8 7 6 5 4 3 2 1

Contents

The Fourth of July: Independence Day / 4

Activity Section

Fireworks Dance / 28

Balloon Fireworks / 30

Real Fireworks Safety Tips / 31

Quill Pen and Cranberry Ink / 32

Patriotic Paper / 34

Red, White, and Blue Fruit Kabobs / 36

Tricorn Hat Serving Bowl / 38

Chocolate Flags / 39

Liberty Bell Noisemaker / 40

Sun Spangled Banner / 42

"T" Party / 44

Stamp Act Stationery / 45

Songs / 46

You're a Grand Old Flag / 46

America, the Beautiful / 47

God Bless America / 47

Yankee Doodle Dandy / 48

The Fourth of July: Independence Day

Independence Day, celebrated on July 4th each year, is one of the most patriotic holidays in the United States! We look forward to this special day so we can celebrate with picnics, barbecues, parades, and we especially enjoy the displays of fabulous fireworks! Many Americans proudly fly the American flag from poles and porches, and politicians often mount bandstands to take this opportunity to say "just a few words" to the Americans they serve. But what were the events that led up to this special holiday? The story of the adoption of the Declaration of Independence on July 4, 1776 is an exciting one, as are the celebrations that followed year after year until today.

As early as the 1600s, when people from far-away lands began to settle in the New World, trouble between the American colonies and their mother country, Great Britain, had been brewing. Colonists in the thirteen colonies along the east coast of North America gathered together, perhaps in schoolhouses or other public meeting places. We can imagine what could have been said at one of these gatherings.

New Orleans

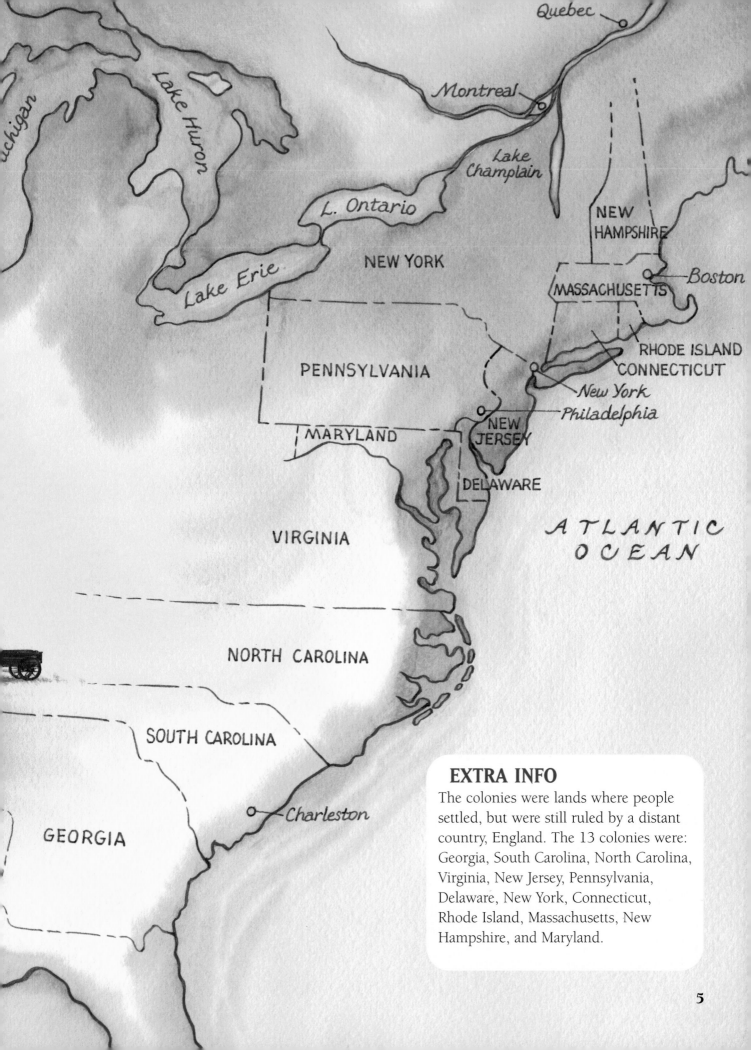

Quebec

Montreal

Lake Champlain

Michigan

Lake Huron

Lake Erie

L. Ontario

NEW YORK

NEW HAMPSHIRE

Boston

MASSACHUSETTS

PENNSYLVANIA

RHODE ISLAND

CONNECTICUT

New York

Philadelphia

NEW JERSEY

MARYLAND

DELAWARE

VIRGINIA

ATLANTIC OCEAN

NORTH CAROLINA

SOUTH CAROLINA

Charleston

GEORGIA

EXTRA INFO

The colonies were lands where people settled, but were still ruled by a distant country, England. The 13 colonies were: Georgia, South Carolina, North Carolina, Virginia, New Jersey, Pennsylvania, Delaware, New York, Connecticut, Rhode Island, Massachusetts, New Hampshire, and Maryland.

"It is all too unfair," shouted one of the colonists. "We left England to find a new life, a new start, a new freedom. We have worked long and hard and faced many dangers to try to achieve this goal. We're tired of the British taking over our lives with their rules, laws, and especially their taxes!"

Another man stood up, knocking his chair over in his anger.

"Our taxes go right to King George in Britain, and yet we have no say in our own government. This must change!"

A third man rose from his chair.

"We must all unite. All thirteen colonies must come together to speak strongly to King George so that we can become free and independent and no longer be under British rule. We will spread the word throughout the colonies. There must be an end to the buying of English goods to help weaken their hold on us."

The crowd shouted in agreement. While there were some in every colony who were against the idea of independence, most of the colonists would band together. On some village greens they raised liberty poles as a sign that they wanted freedom. Soon, people all over the colonies stopped buying English goods.

EXTRA INFO
The Sons of Liberty was a group started by Samuel Adams to protest British taxes. They put up liberty poles, often in the center of town, and flew their flags from the poles; the flags had nine vertical stripes of red and white. Townspeople would gather around the pole to express their feelings about British rule.

EXTRA INFO
England is one of the countries in Great Britain, then ruled by King George. The "English" can also be called the "British."

However, their work was far from over. As the unrest continued to grow in the colonies, King George sent extra troops to help control a possible rebellion. On March 5, 1770, a crowd threw rocks and oyster shells at some British soldiers marching by in their red uniforms.

"Go back to Britain, you lobsters!"

"You are all a bunch of bloody backs," shouted a colonist.

The soldiers fired their guns, killing four men and a boy. News of this incident spread quickly throughout the colonies, and it came to be known as the "Boston Massacre."

The unrest continued, and the British merchants were losing money. The "Boston Tea Party" incident was yet another rebellion against King George's taxation. The colony of Massachusetts was placed under strict military rule. British soldiers could be seen everywhere!

EXTRA INFO
Samuel Adams and others from Boston dressed as American Indians and dumped a cargo of the British-owned India Tea Company into the water to protest the new tea tax and other offenses.

9

The secret meetings to plot against the King continued as the patriots of the rebellion took center stage: John and Samuel Adams, John Hancock, Paul Revere and many others. Finally, in September of 1774, delegates from the colonies (chosen by the people), traveled to Philadelphia to attend a meeting called the *First Continental Congress*. They drew up a list of complaints against the King which became the first writing of a document that would separate the colonies from England.

EXTRA INFO

At that meeting, John Henry cried out: "Give me liberty, or give me death!" Those words have become very famous!

The call to battle was upon them. In April of 1775, the Revolutionary War began with General George Washington in command of the Continental Army. This was the colonists' war for independence and freedom. The battle lasted for eight years and was finally won by the colonies that would later become the United States.

In June of 1776, while the war raged, the colonists sent delegates to the *Second Continental Congress* in Philadelphia. They decided that they must end all ties with the British and create an independent government. With Thomas Jefferson as the writer, and with the help of others on the committee, they made a formal declaration of independence stating their resolve to be free forever from British rule. The first person to sign the declaration was John Hancock, the president of the Continental Congress. He said he signed it "with a great flourish so that King George can read it without spectacles."

FUN FACTS

To this day, to "put your John Hancock" on a piece of paper means to sign your name. Also, "spectacles" are now called "eye glasses."

EXTRA INFO

The Declaration stated that all men were "created equal," and that all of them had a right to "life, liberty, and the pursuit of happiness."

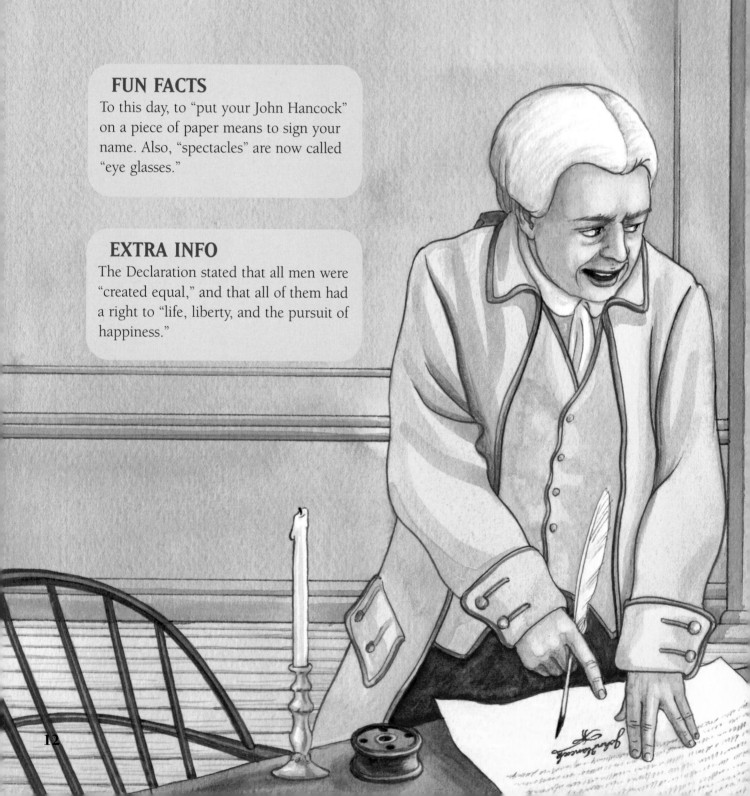

The patriotic words of the declaration stated that the United States of America had the right to form their own government, which could make rules and laws for their people. This government was also to be chosen by the people. If it was not a good government, the people had a right to say so and to change it.

The Delegates took a final vote late in the afternoon of July Fourth. A story is told that on the Fourth of July, a boy had been waiting all day to give a signal to an old bell ringer up in the tower. When Congress had voted, the boy called, "Ring! Ring!" The Liberty Bell rang out…Liberty to all the people!

EXTRA INFO

The Liberty Bell was rung at every important national event until 1835, when the great bell cracked. Since then, the bell has been on display in Independence Hall in Philadelphia, but has never rung again.

One year later, on July 4, 1777, Philadelphia marked Independence Day by celebrating with bonfires, bells, and fireworks. There was lots of noise! Bells rang all day and ships fired their cannons to salute the thirteen colonies. Warships in Philadelphia fired a thirteen gun salute in honor of the thirteen United States. Soldiers stationed in Philadelphia paraded through the streets. At night bonfires were lit and fireworks exploded. Many people put lighted candles in their windows to show their support for the Revolutionary War. Citizens even pulled down a statue of King George and threw pictures of him on bonfires. As word slowly spread to other colonies, other celebrations were held.

FUN FACTS

It took much time for the news of the Declaration to reach all thirteen states. Men on horseback carried the news. They put copies of the Declaration in their saddlebags and rode far and fast to deliver the news of freedom! George Washington read the Declaration to his army.

By the early 1800s, Fourth of July celebrations were really taking shape. The fun and noisy customs eventually spread to many towns, where the day was marked with parades, speeches, picnics, contests, games, military displays, and fireworks. Then, as now, marching bands played patriotic music.

EXTRA INFO

It wasn't until 1941 that Congress declared July 4th a national holiday.

FUN FACTS

Did you ever wonder where Uncle Sam came from? A man named Sam Wilson dealt army supplies during the War of 1812. He was called Uncle Sam by many people and someone said jokingly that the initials U.S. (for United States) that were stamped on each barrel of supplies really stood for "Uncle Sam." Soon the expression became popular, as soldiers talked about fighting Uncle Sam's war. He probably looksd nothing like the tall, thin, bearded figure in striped clothes that was later drawn, but his name is still famous today.

FUN FACTS

The American flag is the only one in the world that has a national anthem or song written about it— "The Star-Spangled Banner."

Our nation now had many patriotic symbols: the Liberty Bell, the American flag, fireworks, patriotic music, picnics, Uncle Sam, and more.

On the Fourth of July, the American flag flies from homes and many public buildings. Each part of the flag's design has a special meaning. The white stars on the blue background stand for the states in the Union. As the numbers of states in the nation increased, so did the number of stars on the flag. In 1818, Congress realized that adding new stripes for each new state would make the flag too large. It was decided that the flag would always have just thirteen stripes, to represent the thirteen original colonies. From 1777 until today, most Americans have felt great pride to see our flag waving majestically on the Fourth of July. Some people simply call the flag the "Red, White, and Blue."

It just wouldn't be much of a July 4th celebration without fireworks! People have celebrated special events with fireworks for hundreds of years, but no one knows who invented them. Ancient Chinese used them often, and it is thought that Marco Polo, the Italian explorer, brought them back to Europe.

Because fireworks contain explosives, they have always been dangerous to handle. Throughout history, there have been many injuries and even deaths caused by them. Today, fireworks are illegal for us to buy in most parts of the country. Only the experts who know how to safely handle fireworks are allowed to dazzle us by staging their glorious displays.

EXTRA INFO

Firecrackers (small fireworks) are made by packing black gunpowder into a roll of paper. A fuse is then attached. When the fuse is lit and the flame reaches the powder, the firecracker explodes. Of course, the fireworks we see in aerial displays are much more complicated than this!

Parades are as much a part of the Fourth as fireworks! Marching bands play our favorite patriotic songs. John Philip Sousa, born in 1854, is famous for many popular marches, such as "Stars and Stripes Forever." George M. Cohan, born in 1878, wrote many patriotic songs, amongst them a favorite, "Yankee Doodle Dandy."

Of course, the most familiar patriotic songs are played—"America the Beautiful" and "The Star-Spangled Banner."

Parades now include marching baseball teams, baton twirlers, high school marching bands and those ever-present politicians, waving from slow-moving cars! Fathers lift little ones onto their shoulders to get a better view, while bigger kids munch popcorn and wave small flags.

FUN FACTS
"Yankee Doodle Dandy" lyrics
I'm a Yankee Doodle Dandy,
A Yankee Doodle do or die.
A real live nephew of my Uncle Sam's,
Born on the Fourth of July.

Back in 1777, the first Fourth of July party was held indoors in Philadelphia. Before long, the feasting part of the celebration moved outdoors, and by the middle of the 19th century, the Fourth of July picnic had become a tradition across the country. Families packed picnic baskets filled with crispy fried chicken, potato salad, pickles, and deviled eggs. There was plenty of lemonade and homemade pies and ice cream for dessert. The baskets were loaded into the family buggy and they were off to the picnic grove!

TRY THIS! Make some July 4th "deviled eggs!"

Hard boil eggs
Cut them in half lengthwise and remove the yolks
Mash the yolks with mayonnaise, mustard, chopped celery, salt, and pepper.
Stuff the mixture back into the eggs and sprinkle with paprika, the "devilish" spice!   YUM!

By the late 1800s, the holiday might include games like tug-of-war over a two-foot-deep mud hole. The children might chase a greased pig! Young and old competed in sack races and watermelon-eating contests.

Today, many people still pack picnic baskets, but they climb into cars, not buggies, and head for picnic grounds, beaches, or backyard barbecues. Deviled eggs are still a treat! Games might include baseball or football instead of pig-chasing, but there still may be sack races and eating contests!

While many Fourth of July customs have not changed much since the earliest celebrations, some communities across the nation have developed their own special traditions. Celebrants in Seward, Alaska take part in a six-mile foot race to the top of a mountain and back! The citizens of Lititz, Pennsylvania have spent their winters since 1818 making thousands of candles so that the children of the town can light them during a special "Festival of Candles," the night of July 4th.

FUN FACTS

On July 4th, 1976, the country marked America's 200th birthday. In Washington, D.C., 33 tons of fireworks were exploded in the sky above the Washington monument. In New York, tall ships from all over the world sailed up the Hudson River.

Each new Independence Day gives us a chance to show our love for our country. The first July 4th celebration came about after many arguments and battles. Today, there may still be arguments on the Fourth, but we are free to voice our differences and to continue to strive for the goals that were set forth in the Declaration of Independence and say, "Liberty to all the people!"

Activity Section

by Ann D. Koffsky

A note to kids and their parents: Many of these crafts involve materials that should only be handled with adult supervision. This includes scissors and especially cooking utensils. Please exercise caution, and make this Fourth of July a happy and a safe holiday! Each activity has a *firecracker* next to its name. The more *firecrackers* pictured, the more complex the activity (1 is easiest, 4 is hardest).

Fireworks Dance

An Independence Day version of "Freeze Dance."

You will need:
Lots of bubble wrap with big bubbles
Duct tape or masking tape
Recording of any upbeat music
Flat surface

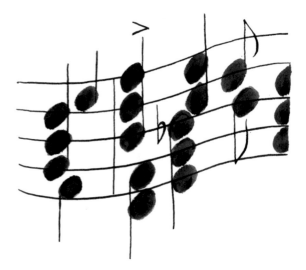

1. Roll out your bubble wrap onto any flat surface, inside or outside.

2. Tape it down so that it won't shift too much from the dancing and jumping.

3. Put your chosen music in a music player.

4. To play, one person starts the music, and everyone else starts dancing near the bubble wrap. Without warning, the person playing the music should suddenly stop it. When they hear the music stop, all dancers have to jump onto the bubble wrap. The dancers should keep jumping to pop as many bubbles as they can until the music starts again. Keep playing until all the "fireworks" are popped!

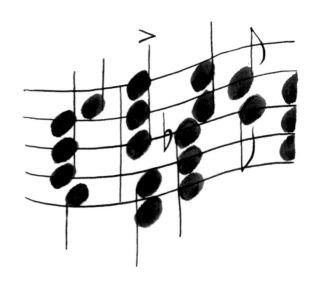

Fun Idea

This works best with a recording of the 1812 Overture by Tchaikovsky. Make sure to stop it at the canon parts!

Balloon Fireworks

An explosion that's safe, loud, and fun.

You will need:
Balloons
Confetti
A good set of lungs
A very sharp pencil

1. Fill each of your balloons with a handful of confetti.
2. Blow them up, and tie them.
3. Have a grown-up stand on a chair, while kids hold up their balloons. The grown-up should pop the balloons with the pencil, and let the confetti "fireworks" fill the air.

Real Fireworks Safety Tips

DO have a grown-up watching nearby.

DO light outdoors, in a safe area.

DO have water nearby.

DO follow all directions.

DO wear eye protection.

DO only light one firework at a time. Keep others away so that they are not accidentally lit.

DO carry fireworks in their original bag or box.

DON'T have young children light fireworks.

DON'T try to relight a firework that didn't work.

DON'T light more than one firework at a time.

DON'T point fireworks at other people or animals.

Quill Pen and Cranberry Ink

Sign your own name the way John Hancock did.

You will need:
A feather (6–8 inches long)
Small knife
1 cup of fresh cranberries
2 tablespoons of water
A pot
Metal strainer
Metal spoon
Clean jar with cover

To make the pen and ink, have a grown-up help you:

Pen:

1. Cut off the tip of the feather.
2. Split through the middle of the shaft, about a 1/2-inch. Cut away one side of the split part.

Ink:

1. Put the cranberries and water in the pot, and bring to a boil. Once the cranberries are softened, let cool.
2. Crush the cranberries with the spoon to release their color.
3. Strain the mixture, and put it in the jar.

To write:

Dip the point of the feather into the ink. Then, lightly tap it on the side of the jar to shake off any extra ink. Start to write, being careful not to press down too hard.

Fun Idea

Write out place cards for your Fourth of July celebration with your new pen. Or, set up the pen and ink at a spot near where your guests arrive. Invite them to use it to sign their names in a guest book.

Patriotic Paper

Looking for something to do while you wait for the fireworks show to start? Here's a craft that will keep you busy. It's easy to take anywhere because it doesn't need glue, paint, or any other messy supplies.

You will need:
1 red, 1 blue, and 1 white 8 1/2" x 11" piece
   of construction paper
Scissors
1 chenille stick

1. Put the blue piece down on a flat surface.

2. Make the red paper slightly smaller than the blue paper by cutting a two-inch strip off the top. Put the red paper in the center of the blue so that you can still see a strip of the blue paper showing at the top and the bottom.

3. Make the white paper slightly smaller than the red by cutting a three-inch strip off the top. Put the white paper in the center of the red paper so that you can see the red peaking through on the top and the bottom.

4. Holding the three papers in position, fold them to create a fan shape, back and forth, accordion style.

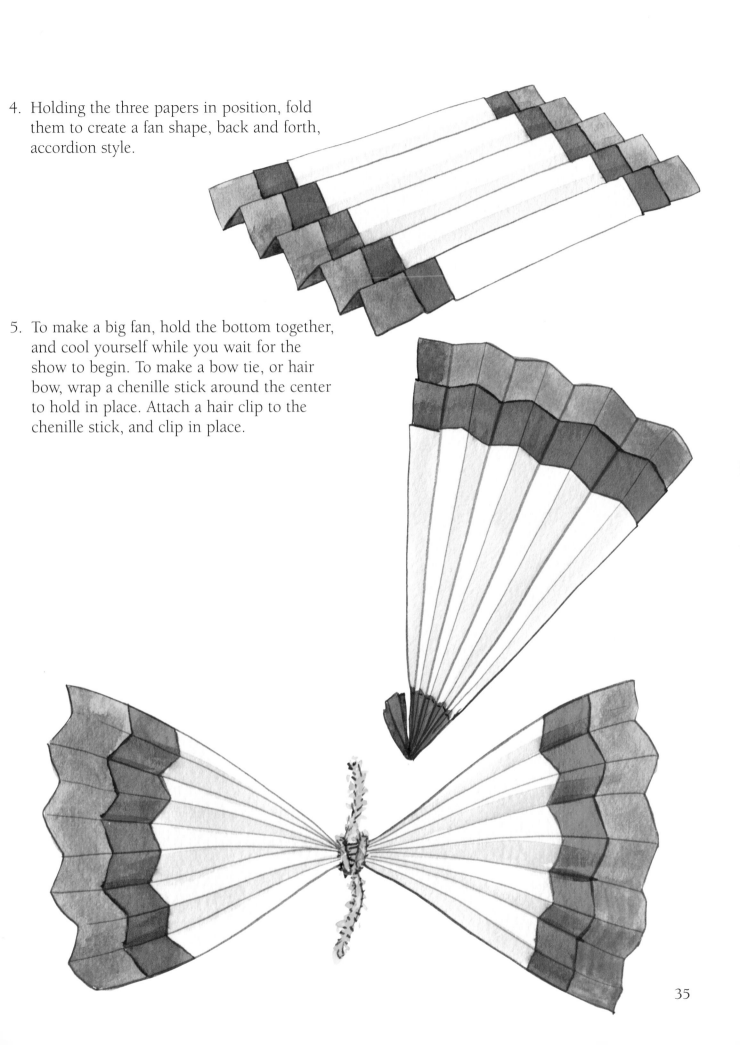

5. To make a big fan, hold the bottom together, and cool yourself while you wait for the show to begin. To make a bow tie, or hair bow, wrap a chenille stick around the center to hold in place. Attach a hair clip to the chenille stick, and clip in place.

Red, White, and Blue Fruit Kabobs

A healthy dessert that's fun to make.

You will need:

Strawberries	1/2 of a medium sized watermelon
Blueberries	Plastic knife
Bananas	Melon baller
Bamboo skewers	Star-shaped cookie cutter

1. Wash the strawberries and blueberries in the sink. Lay the wet fruit on a paper towel and pat dry.

2. Cut the green stems off the strawberries. Peel the bananas.

3. Cut the strawberries and bananas into slices. Use the melon baller to make lots of watermelon balls, but save some of the watermelon for the next step.

4. Cut slices of watermelon, and lay on a flat surface. Use the cookie cutter to make watermelon stars.

5. Slide pieces of fruit onto your skewer in a pattern of red, (strawberry or watermelon) then white (banana) then blue (blueberry). Repeat until each skewer is full.

6. Flip the watermelon over so that the round green side is up.

7. Poke your fruit-filled skewers into the melon rind for a patriotic presentation.

Tricorn Hat Serving Bowl

Include part of the revolutionary uniform at your table.

You will need:
Paper plates
Black crayon or black paint
Stapler

1. Color or paint the bottom of the plate black. Let dry.

2. Fold the sides up to form a triangle. Have a grown-up staple each of the corners in place.

3. Fill with chips, nuts, or candy and serve.

Chocolate Flags

Stars and stripes can be delicious!

You will need:
White chocolate
Food Coloring
Graham Crackers
A new, small paintbrush
Lollipop sticks

1. Divide the white chocolate into three microwavable bowls.

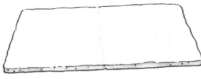

2. With a grown-up, melt the first bowl of chocolate in the microwave.

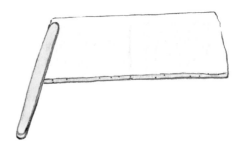

3. Dip your rectangle graham crackers into the "white" bowl so that one side is coated. Lay the crackers on a plate.

4. Put the lollipop stick in on the side of the cracker. To set the stick in place, coat the stick's top half with more white chocolate. Let sit to dry, about 5 minutes.

5. While it is setting, melt the other two bowls of chocolate in the microwave. Stir a few drops of red food coloring into one bowl, and a few drops of blue into the other bowl to make "red" and "blue" chocolate.

6. Take your paintbrush, and paint a flag on the graham cracker. Make a field of blue in the corner, and red stripes. After the blue has dried, you can dot white stars on top.

Fun Idea:

Don't just paint the American flag of today—try painting some of these other historical flags too!

Liberty Bell Noisemaker

Let Freedom Ring at your Fourth of July parade with this noisemaker.

You will need:

A Styrofoam cup with lid
Blue paint
5 small jingle bells (about 1 inch)
3 red craft sticks
Black marker

See-through tape
Several small round bells
Silver glitter pen
Sharp pencil
2 white chenille sticks

1. Hold your craft sticks next to your Styrofoam cup. Compare how they look together to the picture below, and decide if the sticks need to be trimmed. If they do, ask a grown-up to use a kitchen scissors to cut off the ends until the craft sticks are the size you like.

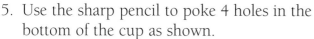

2. Glue the craft sticks together, one on top of the other, as shown.

3. Paint the Styrofoam cup blue. If they aren't already red, paint the craft sticks red.

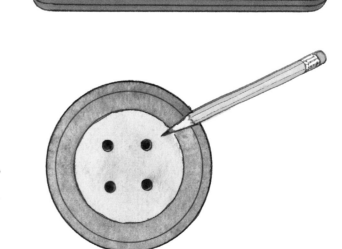

4. Once the paint has dried, flip the cup upside down. Use the black marker to write "Liberty" on your bell, and to draw the famous crack down it's middle. If you want, decorate the bell with the silver glitter, too.

5. Use the sharp pencil to poke 4 holes in the bottom of the cup as shown.

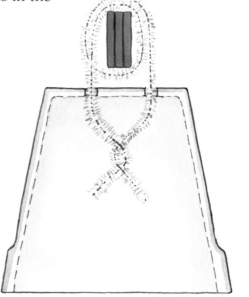

6. Thread each chenille stick through two of the holes, and wrap them around the craft sticks several times. Twist their ends together inside the cup to secure in place.

7. Put your bells inside the cup. Place several pieces of tape around the lid of the cup to fasten it in place.

8. Place tape over the ends of the craft sticks so that any sharp edges are covered.

9. Shake to let freedom ring!

Sun Spangled Banner

A great decoration for your door, playroom, or backyard.

You will need:

Red and blue construction paper
Long string of yarn
Scissors

Restickable glue / or restickable
tape
Glue stick
Sunny weather

1. Fold a piece of construction paper in half.

2. Cut out a triangle, with the base of the triangle on the fold of the paper.

3. Open the triangle, so that it is now a diamond shape.

4. From a fresh piece of paper, cut out two stars. Each star should fit onto one triangle.

5. With restickable glue or tape, stick the stars to the triangles.

6. Repeat, and create as many triangles as you need for the size of banner that you want to make.

7. Tape the papers to a sunny window, for about a week. Then, peel off the stars. The paper around the stars will have faded, leaving a star-shaped sun print.

8. Fold the papers over the yarn. Glue the back of the triangles together.

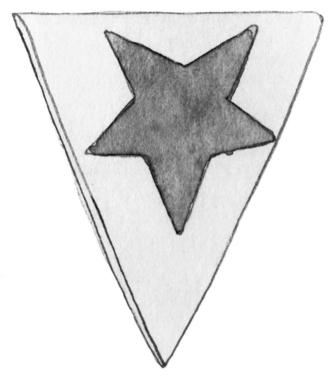

"T" Party

Dump tea—or in this case, T's—into your kiddie pool.

You will need:
Several packs of rectangular kitchen sponges
A good scissors

1. Cut off two rectangles from your sponge to make it into a letter.

2. Repeat to make enough T's, and add them to a kiddie pool filled with water. Younger children will love squeezing the sponges.

Fun Idea

Put cups, plastic pitchers, and small watering cans in the pool and have a real "tea party" in the water.

44

Stamp Act Stationery

The Stamp Act required all American colonists to pay a tax on every piece of printed paper they used. This angered the colonists because it was the first time tax was used to raise money. Stay in touch with this Fourth of July stationery that reminds us of the Stamp Act.

You will need:
White or yellow paper
Rubber stamps in the shapes of stars, stripes, flags, or other holiday icons
Red and blue ink pads
Envelope

1. Cut your paper to 6-1/2 x 9 inches, or to any size that you want your stationery to be.

2. Use your rubber stamps to create a pattern around the border of the front of your paper. After that dries, decorate the back of the paper.

3. You can also rubber stamp your envelope, but be sure to leave space to write the address.

4. Write your message in the empty space, and seal it in your decorated envelope. Put a real stamp on the outside.

Songs

You're a Grand Old Flag

by George M. Cohan

You're a grand old flag,
You're a high flying flag
And forever in peace may you wave.
You're the emblem of
The land I love,
The home of the free and the brave.

Ev'ry heart beats true
'neath the Red, White and Blue,
Where there's never a boast nor brag.
Should auld acquaintance be forgot,
Keep your eye on the grand old flag.

America, the Beautiful

O beautiful for spacious skies,
For amber waves of grain,
For purple mountain majesties
Above the fruited plain!
America! America!
God shed his grace on thee
And crown thy good with brotherhood
From sea to shining sea!

O beautiful for pilgrim feet
Whose stern impassioned stress
A thoroughfare of freedom beat
Across the wilderness!
America! America!
God mend thine every flaw,
Confirm thy soul in self-control,
Thy liberty in law!

God Bless America

God Bless America,
Land that I love.
Stand beside her, and guide her
Thru the night with a light from above.

From the mountains, to the prairies,
To the oceans, white with foam.
God bless America, My home sweet home.

Yankee Doodle Dandy

Yankee Doodle went to town, a-riding on a pony;
Stuck a feather in his cap and called it macaroni.

Yankee Doodle keep it up, Yankee Doodle dandy,
Mind the music and the step and with the girls be handy.

Father and I went down to camp along with Captain Gooding
And there we saw the men and boys, as thick as hasty pudding.

There was Colonel Washington, upon a strapping stallion,
A-giving orders to his men, I guess there was a million.

And there I saw a cannon barrel as big as
mother's basin,
And every time they touched it off they
scampered like the nation.